I Love You with All My Hearts

Written and Illustrated by

Sally Huss

The many ways a mother loves her child

Tommy NELSON

www.tommynelson.com

A Division of Thomas Nelson, Inc.
www.ThomasNelson.com

Published in Nashville, Tennessee, by Tommy Nelson®, a Division of Thomas Nelson, Inc.

Scriptures quoted from the *International Children's Bible®*, *New Century Version®*, copyright © 1986, 1988, 1999 by Tommy Nelson®, a division of Thomas Nelson, Inc. Nashville, Tennessee 37214. Used by permission.

ISBN: 1400305225

Printed in China
04 05 06 07 MTI 9 8 7 6 5 4 3 2 1

For the ones I love with all my hearts:
Michael, Kaitie, and MacKenzie

There are many ways to love
and many ways of love
That you may not have thought of.

Within each person,
   there is a heart for every job or task
      For which a heart
         could possibly be asked.

Here are some of the
   ways I have loved you . . .
And the ways I still do.

When you were a baby,
I gave you baths and kept you dry.
I fed you when you
were hungry
and soothed you
when you'd cry.

I made you wear jackets
and hats on cold days
And fixed you chicken soup
on days when a
cold stays.

There was always a bandage
for a scratch or a bump
And a hug from your mother
when your throat got a lump.

I made sure you had plenty of sleep
and lots of fresh air.
These were the ways I loved you.
These were my hearts of . . . Care.

Then there were times of joy.
You were so full of fun
for such a little one.

You liked to be tickled
from your head to your toes.

And you liked to dress up
in funny old clothes.

You dared the ocean to catch you
when we were at the beach.
And when it did,
you would let out the loudest screech!

A ride on Boulder Mountain
    brought screams and squeals
    and giggles long after.

These were the ways I loved you.
These were my hearts of . . . Laughter.

Now and then there were hard times,
   which brought tears sometimes.
When we had to move
   and you said goodbye,

As you hugged your best friend,
   I thought I would cry.

And as we left our old home
    with all of its memories too,
I knew this was hard on you.

I later saw the disappointment in your eyes when you realized,

We did not have the money
to buy a bike—
we found one to borrow.

These were the ways I loved you.
These were my hearts of . . . Sorrow.

Happily you have learned
    to share your games and toys
With the neighborhood
    girls and boys.

And when your grandfather came to stay,
You even figured out a game
for him to play.

Then you surprised us all at Christmastime,
as you stood upon the stage,
Playing the Christmas angel
and acting well beyond your age.

Your grandmother and I
    were so touched, we cried.
These were the ways I loved you.
These were my hearts of . . . Pride.

Times of peacefulness
found their way into our lives,
Often when you
were about to close your eyes.

At night we spoke of true things,
of important things,
Of God's love,
and blessings from above.

There were quiet picnics under trees,
When we watched the ants
and studied leaves.

And after lunch,
    when all the work was done,
I looked down on you,
    my sleeping one,
    an arm around your lamb of fleece.
These were the ways I loved you.
These were my hearts of . . . Peace.

For these reasons and more—
    including all life's other parts—
I want you to know
    that now and forever,

I love you with all my hearts!